Nuts

THE LITTLE BOOK OF
NUTS
JOKES

THIS IS A CARLTON BOOK

Published by Carlton Books
20 Mortimer Street
London W1T 3JW

ISBN 978-1-84732-079-7

1 3 5 7 9 10 8 6 4 2

Printed in Singapore

The jokes in this book first appeared in
The Nuts Joke Book

Nuts

THE LITTLE BOOK OF
NUTS
JOKES

CARLTON
BOOKS

From the readers of NUTS

If it works for you...

A woman spots a little old man sitting happily on a park bench and wanders over for a chat. "I can't help but notice how happy you look," she says.

"What's your secret?"

"Well," replies the man, "I smoke, drink, eat junk food all day and don't exercise..."

"Wow!" replies the woman. "How old are you?"

"Twenty-three."

Nuts

That's my girl

Bruce is driving over the Sydney Harbour Bridge one day when he sees his girlfriend, Sheila, about to throw herself off.

Bruce slams on the brakes and yells, "Sheila, what the hell d'ya think you're doing?"

Sheila turns around with a tear in her eye and says, "G'day, Bruce. Ya got me pregnant and so now I'm gonna kill meself."

Bruce gets a lump in his throat when he hears this.

"Strewth, Sheila. Not only are you a great shag, but you're a real sport, too!"

Sick as a parrot

Back in the day, Raul, Ronaldo and Beckham were all in Real Madrid's canteen, eating their packed lunches. Raul looked at his and said, "Tapas again! If I get tapas one more time, I'm jumping off the top of the Bernabeu."

Ronaldo opened his lunchbox and exclaimed, "Burritos! If I get burritos again, I'll do the same."

Beckham opened his lunchbox and said, "Ham and cheese again. If I get a ham and cheese sandwich one more time, I'm jumping too."

The next day, Raul opened his lunchbox, saw some tapas and jumped to his death. Then Ronaldo opened his lunchbox, saw a burrito and jumped too.

Nuts

Finally, Beckham opened his lunchbox, saw some ham and cheese sandwiches and followed the others in a fatal plunge.

At the funeral, Raul's wife was weeping. She said, "If I'd known how tired he was of tapas, I never would have given it to him again."

Ronaldo's wife also wept and said, "I could have given him tacos or enchiladas! I didn't realise he hated burritos so much."

Everyone turned to Victoria Beckham, dressed in black Versace.

"Hey, don't look at me," said Posh. "David made his own lunch."

 Nuts

Sick joke

Two buckets of sick are walking down the street.

One bursts into tears.

"What's the matter?" asks the other.

He replies, "This is where I was brought up."

Nuts

Keep it in the family

What did the redneck say to his girlfriend after breaking up with her?

"Can we still be cousins?"

Last respects

Two guys are golfing on a course that is right next to a cemetery.

After they tee off, one of the golfers notices that there is a funeral procession sombrely passing by. He takes off his hat and places it over his heart. When the funeral is over, the other golfer asks, "Why did you do that?" The man replies, "Well, we were married for almost 40 years. It's the least I could do."

Nuts

Why, you little...

A guy is driving down the road at 100mph singing, "Twenty-one today, twenty-one today!" Soon, a cop pulls him over and says, "Because it's your birthday, I'll let you off."

Despite the cop's warning, the guy screeches off and is soon doing a ton down the road again. The cop, in hot pursuit, then sees the man mow down a traffic warden. Suddenly, the man starts singing, "Twenty-two today, twenty-two today!"

Body language

BB King's wife wants to surprise him for his birthday, so she goes to a tattoo parlour and has a big 'B' tattooed on each of her buttocks.

When BB gets home later that night, he opens the door to find his wife naked and bent over showing off her new tattoos. BB can't believe his eyes and screams, "Who the hell's Bob?"

Legend in his own lifetime

An artist asks a gallery-owner if there's been any interest in his paintings recently.

"I have good news and bad news," the gallery owner tells him. "The good news is a gentleman enquired about your work and wondered if it would appreciate in value after your death. When I told him it would, he bought all 15 of your paintings."

"That's great," the artist says. "What's the bad news?"

"He was your doctor."

Balance

How do you tell if a redneck's married?

There are tobacco-spit stains on both sides of the truck.

Nuts

Pump me up

How is sex like air?

It's not a big deal unless you're not getting any.

Law of the jungle

A missionary has spent years teaching agriculture and 'civilization' to some people in a distant land. One day, he wants to start teaching them English. So he takes the tribal chief and points at a tree.

"Tree," says the missionary.

"Tree," mimics the chief.

The holy man then points to a rock.

"Rock," he says.

"Rock," copies the chief.

All of a sudden, they come upon two people having sex in the bushes. Embarrassed, the missionary blurts out that they are 'riding a bike'. Then the chief pulls out his blowpipe and shoots the two people.

"What are you doing?" yells the missionary. "I've spent all this time civilizing you, and you turn around and do this!"

"My bike," says the chief.

Keep on running

A man is ordered by his doctor to lose 75lb due to serious health risks. Desperate, he signs up for a guaranteed weight loss programme. The next day a voluptuous 19-year-old girl arrives, dressed in nothing but running shoes and a sign round her neck, which reads, "If you can catch me, you can have me!" He chases her and, after catching her up, has his way with her. After a few days of this, he is delighted to find he has lost weight and orders a harder programme. The next day, an even sexier woman turns up, wearing nothing but running shoes and the same sign. After five days of her, he decides to go for the company's hardest programme. "Are you sure?"

Nuts

asks the representative on the phone. "This is our most rigorous programme." "Absolutely," he replies. The next day there's a knock at the door and standing there is a muscular guy wearing nothing but pink running shoes and a sign around his neck that reads, "If I catch you, you're mine."

Playing around

One day, a man came home early from work and was greeted by his wife dressed in very sexy lingerie and high heels.

"Tie me up," she purred, "and you can do anything you want."

So he tied her up and went golfing.

Nuts

The spirit is willing, but...

One afternoon, an elderly couple are relaxing in front of the TV. Suddenly, the woman is overcome with lust and says to her husband, "Let's go upstairs and make love." "Steady on," he replies. "I can't do both."

Wise words

The teacher had given her class an assignment. She'd asked her pupils to get their parents to tell them a story that had a moral at the end of it. "So what have you got for me, Johnny?" she asks one pupil sitting at the back of the class.

"Well," replies Johnny. "My mum told a story about my dad.

Dad was a pilot in Desert Storm and his plane got hit. He had to bail out over enemy territory, and all he had was a small flask of whiskey, a pistol and a survival knife. He drank the whiskey on the way down, so it wouldn't fall into enemy hands, and then his parachute landed right in the middle of 20 enemy

Nuts

troops. He shot 15 of them with the gun, until he ran out of bullets, killed four more with the knife, until the blade broke, and then he killed the last one with his bare hands."

"Good heavens!" said the horrified teacher. "What kind of moral did your mum teach you from that horrible story?"

The boy replied: "Stay the hell away from Dad when he's been drinking."

Been good?

Two prostitutes are talking after the Christmas holidays.

"What did you ask Santa Claus to give you?" asks one.

"Hundred quid, as usual," replies the other.

Bite me

What's brown and black, and looks good on a lawyer?
  A doberman.

Nuts

Grave situation

A man comes home from work to find his dog with the neighbour's pet rabbit in its mouth. The rabbit is dead and the man panics. He thinks the neighbours are going to hate him, so he takes the dirty, chewed-up rabbit into the house, gives it a bath, blow-dries its fur and puts it back into the neighbour's cage, hoping they'll think it died of natural causes. A few days later, the neighbour asks the guy, "Did you hear that Fluffy died?" The man stammers and says, "Um, no. What happened?" The neighbour replies, "We just found him dead in his cage one day, but the weird thing is that the day after we buried him, we went outside and someone had dug him up, given him a bath and put him back into the cage. There must be some really sick people out there!"

Mutual satisfaction

A man drives his date up to Lovers' Lane and parks up.

"I have to be honest with you," the woman says as the man makes his move. "I'm a prostitute."

The man thinks about this for a bit and decides he's OK with it. He agrees to pay her £25 in advance and they get down to business.

After they finish, the man says, "Now, I should be honest, too. I'm a taxi driver and it's going to cost you £25 to get back into town."

Unless it was a putter

A golf club walks into a local bar and asks the barman for a pint of beer.

"Sorry, mate, but I'm not supposed to serve you," says the barman.

"Why not?" says the golf club.

"You'll be driving later," replies the bartender.

Nuts

Ugly all over

Why do bagpipers walk when they play?
  To get away from the sound.

All the fun

What happens to someone fired from a job at a fairground?

They sue for funfair dismissal.

Going bananas

A gorilla walks into a bar and orders a pint of lager. The barman charges him five quid and, after looking at him for a while, says, "Do you know, you're the first gorilla we've had in here for ages?"

"I'm not bloody surprised," replies the gorilla, "at a fiver a pint."

Cut to the chase

A man walks into an antiques shop. After a while, he chooses a brass rat and brings it to the counter.

"That will be £10 for the brass rat and £1,000 for the story behind it," says the owner.

"Thanks, but I'll pay the £10 and pass on the story," replies the man.

So the man buys the brass rat and leaves the shop. As he walks down the street, he notices all sorts of rats following him. The further he walks, the more rats follow. He walks down to the pier and still more rats come out and follow him. So he decides to walk out into the water and all the rats drown. Afterwards, he goes back to the shop.

Nuts

"Ah-ha, you're back!" says the owner. "You've come back for the story, right?"

"Nope," says the man. "You got any brass lawyers?"

The cruel sea

The first mate on a ship decided to celebrate his birthday with some contraband rum. Unfortunately, he was still drunk the next morning. Realising this, the captain wrote in the ship's log: "The first mate was drunk today."

"Captain, please don't let that stay in the log," the mate said. "This could add months or years to my becoming a captain myself."

"Is it true?" asked the captain, already knowing the answer.

"Yes, it's true," the mate said.

"Then, if it's true, it has to go in the log. That's the rule," said the captain, sternly.

Nuts

A few weeks later, it was the first mate's turn to make the log entries. The first mate wrote: "The ship seems in particularly good shape. The captain was sober today."

Number-crunching

Donald Rumsfeld is giving the President his daily briefing on Iraq. He concludes by saying: "Yesterday, seven Brazilian soldiers were killed in an ambush."

"Oh, no! That's terrible!" the President exclaims.

His staff sit stunned at this display of emotion, nervously watching as the President sits, head in hands.

Finally, the President looks up and asks, "Um... how many is a brazillion, exactly?"

Fruit cocktail

Patient: "Doctor, I've got a strawberry stuck up my bum."

Doctor: "I've got some cream for that."

What a waterfowl world

Three women die together in an accident and go to Heaven.

When they get there, Saint Peter says, "We only have one rule here in Heaven; don't step on the ducks."

Sure enough, there are ducks everywhere in Heaven. It is almost impossible not to step on a duck and, although they try their best to avoid them, the first woman accidentally steps on one. Along comes Saint Peter with the ugliest man she ever saw.

Saint Peter chains them together and says, "Your punishment for stepping on a duck is to spend eternity chained to this ugly man."

Nuts

The next day, the second woman steps on a duck and along comes Saint Peter. With him is another extremely ugly man. He chains them together with the same admonition as he gave the first woman.

The third woman, having observed all this, is very, very careful where she steps. She manages to go months without stepping on any ducks, but one day Saint Peter comes up to her with the most handsome man she's ever seen and, silently, he chains them together. The happy woman says, "Wonder what I did to deserve being chained to you for all of eternity?"

The guy says, "I don't know about you, but I stepped on a duck."

Nuts

Your sins are forgiven you

A nun goes to confession. "Forgive me, Father," she says.

"I used horrible language this weekend."

"Go on," the priest says.

"Well," the nun continues, "I was playing golf and hit an incredible drive, but it hit a phone line and fell short after about only 100 yards."

"And you swore?" the priest asks.

"No," the nun says. "After that, a squirrel ran out and stole my ball."

"You swore then?" the priest asks.

"Well, no," the nun says. "Then, an eagle swooped down and grabbed the squirrel in his talons. As they flew away, the squirrel dropped my ball."

"Then you swore?" the father asks.

"No," she continues. "The ball fell on a big rock, rolled on to the green and stopped six inches from the hole."

The priest is silent for a moment and then finally says, "You missed the f**king putt, didn't you?"

Suspicious minds

A worried man calls up his best mate in a panic. "I really need your advice, pal. I'm desperate and I don't know what to do."

His friend replies, "Sure, I'll try and help. What's wrong?"

The worried man explains: "For some time now, I've suspected that my wife may be cheating on me. You know the sort of thing; the phone rings, I answer, someone hangs up."

"That's terrible, mate," says his friend.

"That's not all," continues the worried man. "The other day, I picked up her mobile, just to see what time it was, and she went mental, screaming at me that I should never touch her phone again and that I was checking up on her. So far I haven't confronted her about it. I sort of think, deep down, I don't really want to know the truth. But then, last night, she went out again and I decided to check up on her. I hid behind my car, which I knew would give me a good view of the whole street. That way, I could see which car she got out of on her return. Anyway, it was while I was crouched behind my car that I noticed some rust around the rear wheel arch. So, do you think I should take it into a body repair shop or just buy some of that stuff from Halfords and try to sort it out myself?"

God sees all

During his wedding rehearsal, the groom approached the vicar and said, "Look, I'll give you £100 if you'll change the wedding vows and miss out the 'love, honour and obey' part."

He passed the clergyman the cash and left the church satisfied.

On his wedding day, when it came time for the groom's vows, the vicar looked the young man in the eye and said: "Will you promise to love, honour and obey her every command and wish, serve her breakfast in bed every morning and swear that you will never look at another woman, as long as you both shall live?"

The groom gulped and said in a squeaky voice, "Yes."

He then leaned toward the vicar and hissed through clenched teeth, "I thought we had a deal?"

The vicar looked at the bride. "She made me a better offer."

Sleeping partner

A man gets taken on as a lorry driver at a new company, but as he's about to sign his contract in the boss's office, he says, "I've got one demand. Since you employed me, you've got to hire my mate, Dave, too."

"Who's Dave?" says the boss, surprised at the demand.

"Dave's my driving partner. We're a team. He drives when I sleep and I drive when he sleeps," the new employee says. "OK," says the boss. "Answer this question satisfactorily and I'll hire your mate too.

Nuts

"You're going down a hill, your brakes fail and ahead of you is a bridge with an 18-wheeler jackknifed across it. What would you do?"

"I'd wake Dave up," he replies.

"How the hell's that going to help?" says the boss.

"We've been working together 25 years," explains the new guy, "and he's never seen a wreck like the one we're about to have!"

First things first

A lawyer parks his brand-new Jaguar and, just as he steps out, a truck comes barrelling down the street and tears the driver's door clean off. The lawyer calls 999 and within five minutes the police are on the scene. But before he can start filling in his incident report, the copper is amazed to hear the lawyer screaming about how his new Jag is wrecked beyond repair. When the lawyer finally calms down, the cop shakes his head in disgust. "I can't believe how materialistic you lawyers are," he says. "You're so focused on your possessions that you don't notice anything else."

Nuts

"How can you say such a thing?" the lawyer asks.

"For God's sake, man," the copper yells. "Your left arm is missing from the elbow down! It must have been torn off in the accident."

"Arrgh!" the lawyer cries. "Where's my Rolex?"

Bowl me over

A boy goes to the Jobcentre and says, "I'd like to work in a bowling alley."

"Ten pin?" says the man behind the desk.

"No, permanent," says the boy.

Nuts

Frozen stiff

What do you call 12 naked men sitting on each others' shoulders?

A scrotum pole.

A night to remember

As Claude the hypnotist took to the stage, he announced, "Unlike most stage hypnotists, I intend to hypnotise each and every member of the audience."

Claude then withdrew a beautiful antique pocket watch from his coat. "I want you each to keep your eye on this antique watch. It's a very special watch. It has been in my family for six generations."

He began to swing the watch gently back and forth while quietly chanting, "Watch the watch. Watch the watch. Watch the watch. Watch the watch. Watch the watch..."

Hundreds of pairs of eyes followed the swaying watch – until, unexpectedly, it slipped from Claude's

Nuts

fingers and fell to the floor, breaking into a hundred pieces.

"Sh*t!" exclaimed the hypnotist, loudly. It took three weeks to clean the seats.

Never too old

Bert, 92, and Agnes, 89, are about to get married. They go for a stroll to discuss the wedding and on the way they pass a chemist. Bert suggests they go in.

Bert first asks the pharmacist, "Do you sell heart medication?"

Pharmacist: "Of course."

Bert: "How about medicine for circulation?"

Pharmacist: "All kinds."

Bert: "How about Viagra?"

Pharmacist: "Of course."

Bert: "Do you sell wheelchairs and walkers?"

Pharmacist: "We do – all speeds and sizes."

Bert: "That's brilliant! We'd like to use this shop for our wedding list, please."

Nuts

Swamp thing

A man walks into a pub with his dog on a lead. The landlord says, "That's a weird-looking dog. He's got stumpy legs, he's pink and he doesn't have a tail. I bet my rottweiler could beat him in a scrap." They bet £50 and, out in the backyard, the rottweiler is soon whimpering for mercy.

Another drinker says his pit bull will win and the bet is increased to £100. There's another trip to the backyard and when it's all over the pitbull is cowering behind his owner, who pays up and says, "So what breed is he, anyway?"

The owner says, "Well, until I cut his tail off and painted him pink, he was the same breed as every other alligator."

Georgie girl

Saint George went to a transvestite party and said,
"How do you like me with my drag on?"

Strange link

What do Kermit the Frog and Henry the Eighth have in common?

They both have the same middle name.

Divine protection

Reggie Kray dies and goes to Heaven. At the Pearly Gates, Saint Peter asks his name.

"Kray. Reginald," he replies.

Saint Peter looks him up on the computer and a list of crimes as long as his arm comes up on his database.

Worried, Saint Peter goes to check with God before he can let him in.

"This is no good," says God. "Send him downstairs to Hell."

Saint Peter goes back out to the gates and says, "I'm sorry, Mr Kray, but we can't let you in."

To which Reggie replies, "I don't want to come in. I want £2,000 a week or I'm shutting you down."

Nuts

Geography riddle

What do you call a guy born in Leeds, who grows up in Edinburgh and dies in Liverpool?
  Dead.

Doesn't quite add up

A bank manager in America notices that one of his new cashiers lacks basic arithmetic skills. He calls the new man into his office. "Son, where did you say you studied finance again?" the manager asks.

"Yale, sir," the cashier replies.

"I see," says the bank manager, certain he must have pulled the wrong employee aside. "And what did you say your name was?"

"Yim Yohnson, sir," he replies.

Mission of mercy

A surgeon was relaxing on his sofa one evening when the phone rang. The doctor calmly answered it and heard the familiar voice of a colleague on the other end of the line. "We need a fourth for poker," said the friend.

"I'll be right over," whispered the surgeon.

As he was putting on his coat, his wife asked, "Is it serious?"

"Oh, yes, quite serious," said the surgeon, gravely. "Three doctors are there already!"

Do you have it in pink?

A woman walks into a gun shop and asks the salesman if he can help her pick out a rifle.

"It's for my husband," she explains.

"Did he tell you what calibre to get?" asks the salesman.

"Are you kidding?" she replies. "He doesn't even know I'm going to shoot him."

It's in the bag

A cowboy walks into a bar and orders a whiskey. When the bartender delivers the drink, the cowboy asks, "Where is everybody?" The bartender replies, "They've gone to the hanging." "Hanging? Who are they hanging?" "Brown Paper Pete," the bartender replies. "What kind of a name is that?" the cowboy asks. "Well," says the bartender, "he wears a brown paper hat, brown paper shirt, brown paper trousers and brown paper shoes." "How bizarre," says the cowboy. "What are they hanging him for?" "Rustling," says the bartender.

Nuts

A worthy cause

A driver was stuck in a traffic jam. Suddenly, a man knocked on his window. The driver rolled down his window and asked, "What's up?" The man said excitedly, "President Bush has been kidnapped by terrorists. They will cover him in petrol and burn him if they don't get $10million ransom." The driver asked, "And what do you want me to do?" "Well, we're going from car to car and collecting for the cause," answered the man. "Aha... and how much are people giving?" asked the driver. "Oh, somewhere around one or two gallons."

Nuts

Concentrate

How many kids with Attention Deficit Hyperactivity Disorder does it take to change a light bulb?
   Wanna ride bikes?

Man's best friend

What makes men chase women they have no intention of marrying?

The same urge that makes dogs chase cars they have no intention of driving.

Short back

A man goes into the barbers. The barber asks, "Do you want a crew cut?"

The man replies, "No, thanks, it's just for me."

Two can play that game

Little Johnny and his grandfather have gone fishing. After a while, Grandpa gets thirsty and opens up his cooler for some beer. Little Johnny asks, "Grandpa, can I have some beer, too?" "Can you stick your penis in your arsehole?" Grandpa asks back. "No." "Well, then you're not big enough."

Grandpa then takes out a cigarette and lights up. Little Johnny sees this and asks for a cigarette.

"Can you stick your penis in your arsehole?" Grandpa asks again. "No." "Well, then you're not big enough." Little Johnny gets upset and pulls out some cookies. His grandfather says, "Hey, those cookies look good. Can I have some?" Little Johnny asks, "Can you stick your penis in your arsehole?" Grandpa looks at Johnny and senses his trick, so he says, "Well, of course I can, I'm big enough." Little Johnny then says, "Well, go shag yourself, these are my cookies."

Tune in

What do you get when you cross LSD with a birth control pill?

A trip without the kids.

Sober judgement

A man goes into a lawyer's office and says, "I heard people have sued tobacco companies for giving them lung cancer."

The lawyer says, "Yes, that's perfectly true."

The man says, "Well, I'm interested in sueing someone, too."

The lawyer says, "OK. Who are you talking about?"

The man replies, "I'd like to sue all the breweries for the ugly women I've slept with."

Get literal

A man walks into a record shop and asks, "What have you got by The Doors?"

The owner replies, "A mop and a fire extinguisher."

The right career move

A plumber attended to a leaking tap at a stately home. After a two-minute job, he demanded £75. "Christ, even I don't charge this much and I'm a surgeon!" said the owner.

The plumber replied, "You're right – that's why I switched from surgery to plumbing."

Get it off your chest

An old couple are sitting on the porch one afternoon, rocking in their rocking chairs.

All of a sudden, the old man reaches over and slaps his wife. "What was that for?" she asks. "That's for 40 years of rotten sex!" he replies. His wife doesn't say anything and they start rocking again. All of a sudden, the old lady reaches over and slaps her husband hard across the face. "Well, what was that for?" he asks. "That's for knowing the difference!"

Nuts

Not so sweet

A Jelly Baby goes to the doctor. "Doctor, doctor, I think I've got an STD."

The doctor is surprised, "You can't have an STD, you're a Jelly Baby!"

"But, doctor, I've been sleeping with Allsorts."

Tales from the crypt

Late one night, a young chap was walking home from a club. Most of the streetlights in the area were broken. Suddenly, he heard a strange noise. Startled, he turned and saw a coffin following him. He started to jog, but he heard the coffin speed up after him. Eventually, he made it to his front door, but he knew the coffin was only seconds behind. He dived inside, slamming the front door behind him.

Then, there was a crash as the coffin smashed its way through the front door. In horror, the young lad fled upstairs to the bathroom and locked the door.

With an almighty smash, the bathroom door flew off

its hinges and the coffin stood in its place. Desperate, the young man reached into his bathroom cabinet. He grabbed a bar of Imperial Leather soap and threw it at the coffin, but still it came. He grabbed a can of Lynx deodorant and threw it, but still it came. Finally, he threw some cough mixture. The coffin stopped.

My compliments to the chef

A resident in a posh hotel breakfast room calls the head waiter over one morning.

"Good morning, sir," says the waiter. "What would you like for breakfast today?"

"I'd like two boiled eggs, one of them so undercooked it's runny, and the other so overcooked it's tough and hard to eat. Also, grilled bacon that has been left out so it gets a bit on the cold side; burnt toast that crumbles away as soon as you touch it with a knife; butter straight from the deep freeze so that it's impossible to spread; and a pot of very weak coffee, lukewarm."

"That's a complicated order, sir," says the bewildered waiter. "It might be quite difficult."

The guest replies, "Oh? I don't understand why. That's exactly what I got yesterday."

Nuts

Telling it straight

A teacher says to her class, "I'm going to call on each of you and you're going to tell me what your father does for a living. Tommy, you're first."

Tommy says, "My father's a doctor."

The teacher says, "Jamie, what about you?"

Jamie says, "My father's a lawyer."

Finally, there's one boy left and the teacher says, "Billy, what does your father do?"

Billy replies, "My father's dead, Miss."

Shocked, the teacher says, "I'm so sorry. What did he do before he died?"

Billy says, "He turned purple and collapsed on the dog, Miss."

Nuts

Your own fault

What's the punishment for bigamy?
   Two mothers-in-law.

Mustn't grumble

Morris and his wife, Esther, went to the funfair every year.

And every year, Morris would say, "Esther, I'd like to ride in that helicopter."

Esther always replied, "Yes, it looks fun, Morris, but that helicopter ride is £50 – and £50 is £50."

One year later, Esther and Morris went to the fair again.

Morris said, "Esther, I'm 85 years old. If I don't ride that helicopter now, I might never get another chance."

Esther replied, "That's all very well, Morris, but that helicopter ride is £50 – and £50 is £50."

The pilot overheard the couple. He said, "Folks, I'll make you a deal. I'll take both of you for a ride. If you can stay quiet for the entire ride and not say a word, I won't charge you. But if you say one word, it's £50."

Morris and Esther agreed and up they went. The pilot did all kinds of fancy manoeuvres, but not a word was heard.

He did his daredevil tricks over and over again, but still not a word. When they landed, the pilot turned to Morris and said, "Blimey! I did everything I could to get you to yell out, but you didn't. I'm impressed!"

Morris replied, "Well, I was going to say something when Esther fell out halfway through, but £50 is £50."

Best of friends

Spotting a monkey at the side of the road, a truck driver pulls over, opens the passenger door and asks, "Do you need a lift?" The monkey hops in but, as they drive off, a policeman pulls them over.

"I want you to take that monkey to the zoo," the officer barks.

"Yeah, I suppose that would be the best thing to do with him," the truck driver agrees.

The next day, the policeman sees the monkey sitting in the same truck, so he pulls the trucker over again and says, "I thought I told you to take that monkey to the zoo!"

The trucker replies, "Oh, I did, officer, and we had a great time. Today we're going fishing."

Every home should have one

A man walks into a pub with a small doll in his hand and says to the barmaid, "What's this?"

He then pokes the doll in the stomach and a man in the corner of the pub screams. Without saying a word, the man then leaves.

The next day, the man walks back into the pub at the same time and says to the same barmaid, "What's this?"

He pokes the doll in the stomach as before and, once again, a man in the corner screams.

As the man is about to leave, the barmaid shouts, "I don't know. What is it?"

"Déja voodoo," replies the man.

Baggage allowance

Dave says to Phil, "You know, I reckon I'm about ready for a holiday, only this year I'm gonna do it a little different.

"The last few years, I took your advice as to where to go. Two years ago you said to go to Tenerife; I went to Tenerife and Marie got pregnant. Then last year you told me to go to the Bahamas; I went to the Bahamas and Marie got pregnant again."

Phil says, "So what are you gonna do different this year?"

Dave says, "This year, I'm takin' Marie with me..."

Miss! Miss!

A customer wanted to ask his attractive waitress for a date, but couldn't get her attention. When he was finally able to catch her eye, she quickly looked away.

Finally, he followed her into the kitchen and blurted out his invitation. To his amazement, she said yes. So he asked, "Why have you been avoiding me all this time? You wouldn't even make eye contact with me."

"Oh," replied the waitress, "I just thought you were after more coffee."

0 Lucky man

What do you call a New Zealander with a sheep under one arm and a goat under the other?

Bisexual.

Bird brain

A man follows a woman with a parrot out of a cinema, stops her and says, "I'm sorry to bother you, but I couldn't help noticing that your bird seemed to understand the film. He cried at the right parts and he laughed at the jokes. Don't you find that unusual?"

"I do indeed," she replies. "He hated the book."

Can't I just walk along a line?

A driver was pulled over by a policeman for speeding.

As the officer was writing the ticket, he noticed several machetes in the car. "What are those for?" he asked suspiciously.

"I'm a juggler," the man replied.

"I use those in my act."

"Well, show me," the officer demanded.

The driver got out the machetes and started juggling them, eventually doing seven at one time. Seeing this, the driver of another car passing by said to his passenger, "Remind me never to drink and drive. Look at the test they're giving now."

Nuts

Quick thinking

One fine spring day, a farmer walks through his orchard to a nearby pond, carrying a bucket of fruit. Once there, he spies two sexy young women skinny-dipping. Spotting him, they duck down below the water so that only their heads are visible.

"We're not coming out until you leave!" shouts one of the girls.

Thinking on his feet, the farmer replies: "Oh, I'm not here to see you two – just here to feed the piranhas!"

Monkey business

A man walks into a bar and sees a monkey in a cage.

He asks the bartender, "What does the monkey do?"

The barman says, "I'll show you." He opens the cage door, hits the monkey on the head with a cricket bat and the monkey gives him oral sex.

The man is amazed and the bartender says, "You want to have a go?"

"Definitely," says the man, "just don't hit me so hard with the bat."

Read it and weep

What's black and white and red all over?
  A cow that's just been murdered.

Snap diagnosis

While making his rounds, a doctor points out an X-ray to a group of medical students.

"As you can see," he begins, "the patient has a limp because his left fibula and tibia are radically arched." The doctor turns to one of the students and asks, "What would you do in a case like this?"

"Well," ponders the student, "I suppose I'd limp, too."

I confess

Henry goes to confession and says, "Bless me, Father, for I have sinned. Last night I was with seven different women."

The priest quietly replies, "Take seven lemons, squeeze them into a glass and drink the juice without pausing."

Henry, looking surprised, says, "Will that cleanse me of my sins, Father?"

"No," says the priest, but it'll wipe that stupid grin off your face."

Pulling the wool over your eyes

A ventriloquist is visiting New Zealand when he stumbles across a small village and decides to have some fun.

Approaching a man on his porch patting his dog, he says, "Can I talk to your dog?"

The villager just laughs at him and says, "Are you stupid? The dog doesn't talk."

"Are you sure?" asks the ventriloquist. Turning to the dog, he says: "Hello, mate, how's it going?"

"I'm doin' all right," the dog replies. At this, the villager looks shocked. "Is this your owner?" "Yep," says the dog. "How does he treat you?" asks the ventriloquist. "Really well. He walks me twice a day, feeds me great food and takes me to the lake once a week to play."

"Mind if I talk to your horse?" the ventriloquist asks the villager. The horse tells the ventriloquist that he is also treated pretty well. "I am ridden regularly, brushed down often and kept in a nice barn."

"Mind if I talk to your sheep?" the ventriloquist then asks. In a panic, the villager turns around and shouts: "The sheep's a liar!"

Nuts

It was worth a try

A mild-mannered man is tired of his wife always bossing him around, so he decides to be more assertive.

When he gets home from work, he says to his wife, "From now on, I'm the man of this house. When I come home from work, I want my dinner on the table. Now go upstairs and lay me some clothes on the bed, because I'm going out with the boys tonight. Then draw my bath.

"And, when I get out of the tub, guess who's going to dress me?"

"The undertaker?" she replies.

Nuts

Barking mad

Why couldn't Rover bark?
  Because he was a goldfish.

Shellshock

A man walks into a pub holding a turtle. The turtle has two bandaged legs, a black eye and his shell is held together with duct tape. The landlord asks, "What's wrong with your turtle?" "Nothing," the man responds. "This turtle's very fast. Have your dog stand at the end of the bar. Then go and stand at the other end of the room and call him. Before that mutt reaches you, my turtle will be there." So the landlord, wanting to see this, sets down his dog at one side of the room. Then he goes to the other side and calls him. Suddenly, the guy picks up his bandaged turtle and throws it across the room, narrowly missing the landlord and smashing it into the wall. "Told you!"

Nuts

Fowl story

A man asked a waiter: "I'm just wondering, exactly how do you prepare your chickens?"

"Nothing special, sir. We just tell them straight out that they're going to die."

Bird of pray

A priest walks into a pet shop to buy a bird. The owner beckons him over to a parrot. "This is a special parrot," he says. "If you pull the string on the left leg he recites The Lord's Prayer. Pull the string on his right leg and he recites Genesis." "What if you pull both strings?" asks the priest.

The parrot screams: "Then I fall off my perch, you idiot!"

Of course

Why did the horse win the Nobel Prize?
   Because he was out standing in his field.

The human condition

Two Arabs boarded a flight out of London. One took a window seat and the other sat next to him in the middle seat. Just before take-off, an American sat down in the aisle seat.

After take-off, the American kicked his shoes off and was settling in for the flight when the Arab in the window seat said, "Excuse me. I need to get up and get a Coke."

"Don't get up," said the American, "I'm in the aisle seat. I'll get it for you."

As soon as he left, one of the Arabs picked up the American's right shoe and spat in it.

When the American returned with the Coke, the other Arab said, "That looks good, I'd really like one, too."

The American went to fetch it and, while he was

Nuts

gone, the other Arab picked up his left shoe and spat in it. Once the American returned with the drink, they all sat back and enjoyed the flight.

As the plane was landing, the American slipped his feet into his shoes and knew immediately what had happened.

"Why does it have to be this way?" the American asked out loud. "How long must this go on?"

He turned to look at the two Arabs. "All this distrust between our great nations? All this hatred? All this animosity? All this spitting in shoes and pissing in Cokes?"

VIP treatment

The Pope lands in New York Airport, where a limo is waiting for him. The Pope gets in and says to the limo driver, "Mate, I haven't got a lot left in me. Please may I have an opportunity to drive a limo before I leave this world?" The limo driver thinks about it and agrees. The Pope then proceeds to drive the limo at 105mph down the streets of Manhattan until he's stopped by the police. The Pope winds down the window and gives the usual "Sorry, officer, I didn't know I was speeding" spiel. The cop gets on his radio and calls head office.

"I've pulled over a limo for speeding and it's got a very important passenger," says the cop.

"Who is it? The senator? The president?" asks the commissioner.

"No, much more important than that," replies the cop.

"Who's more important than the president?" scoffs the commissioner.

"I think it's God," says the cop.

"How could it possibly be God, you fool?" asks the commissioner.

"Well," replies the cop. "The Pope is the chauffeur."

Nuts

Watch what you eat

Two men are sitting in the doctor's office. The first man is holding his shoulder in pain, while the second man has ketchup in his hair, fried egg down the front of his shirt and two sausages sticking out of his pockets. After a while, the second man asks the other what happened. "My cat got stuck in a tree," the man says, gripping his arm. I went up after him and fell out. I think I've broken my shoulder. You?"

"Oh, it's nothing serious," the second man replies. "I'm just not eating properly."

Nuts

Fur real

What do you call a bear without a paw?
A bastard.

Your call

A husband and wife are watching *Who Wants To Be A Millionaire?* It gets the husband thinking and he looks over at his wife, winks and says, "Honey, let's go upstairs."

"No," sighs his wife.

The husband looks at her and says, "Is that your final answer?"

"Yes," she replies.

"In that case," smiles hubby, "can I phone a friend?"

Nuts

Gather round

How do you get 500 cows in a barn?
   Put up a sign saying "Bingo".

Snot a problem

A man and a woman are sitting next to one another on a flight to New York. The woman sneezes, takes out a tissue, wipes her nose and then shudders for about ten seconds.

A few minutes later, the woman sneezes again. Once more, she takes a tissue, wipes her nose and then shudders. A few more minutes pass before the woman sneezes and shudders again. Curious, the man says, "I can't help noticing that you keep sneezing and shuddering. Are you OK?"

"I'm so sorry if I disturbed you," says the woman. "I suffer from a condition that means whenever I sneeze, I have an orgasm."

"My God!" says the man. "Are you taking anything for it?"

"Yes," says the woman. "Pepper."

Fleeced

Where do you get virgin wool from?
  Ugly sheep.

Don't call for backup

Did you hear about the new French tank?

It has 14 gears. Thirteen go in reverse and one forward, in case the enemy attacks from behind.

Nuts

I have foreseen it

A worker rings up work and speaks to his boss:

"Hi, boss, I'm sorry but I'm not going to be able to come in for work today."

The boss replies by asking, "What's wrong with you?"

"I have a vision problem," explains the lad.

"Sounds serious," says his boss. "What seems to be the problem?"

"Well," says the worker, "I just don't see myself at work today."

The way they are

Two lawyers are walking down the street, when a beautiful woman walks by. "Boy, I'd like to screw her," says one lawyer.

"Yeah, I would, too," says the other. "But out of what?"

Nuts

Braking the habit

One day, a mechanic was working under a car when some brake fluid accidentally dripped into his mouth. "Wow," said the mechanic to himself. "That stuff tastes good."

The following day, he told his mate about his discovery.

"It tastes great," said the mechanic. "I think I'll try a little more today."

The next day, the mechanic told his mate he'd drunk a pint of the stuff. His friend was worried, but didn't say anything until the next day, when the mechanic revealed he'd drunk two pints.

"Don't you know that brake fluid is toxic? It's really bad for you," said his mate.

"I know what I'm doing," snapped the mechanic. "I can stop any time I want to."

Nuts

Death from above

A woman walks into the kitchen to find her husband stalking around with a fly-swatter.

"What are you doing?" she asks.

"Hunting flies," he replies.

"Oh. Killed any?" she enquires.

"Three males and two females," the husband responds.

Intrigued, she asks, "How can you tell?"

"Easy," the husband replies. "Three were on a beer can and the other two were on the phone."

All mod cons

Proudly showing off his new apartment to some friends late one night, a drunk leads the way to his bedroom. When they get there, they see that there's a big brass gong taking pride of place.

"What's with that gong?" one of the friends asks.

"That's no gong," the drunk replies. "It's a talking clock!"

"Oh yeah? How does it work, then?" the friend asks.

"Watch," the drunk says. He moves to the corner of the room, picks up a hammer and pounds the gong as loudly as he can.

Suddenly, someone on the other side of the wall starts screaming: "What the hell do you think you're doing? It's three o'clock in the bloody morning!"

It's enough to wake the dead!

A funeral service is being held for a woman who has just died. As the pallbearers are carrying out the casket, they accidentally bump into a wall. Hearing a faint moan from inside, the woman's husband opens the casket to find that his wife is actually alive! She dies again ten years later and her husband has to arrange another funeral. This time, when the casket is carried towards the door, the husband yells, "Watch out for the bloody wall!"

Nuts

Bargain

Why do women love men who have been circumcised?
They can't resist something with 20 per cent off!

That certain something

A young primary school teacher decides to teach her class a new word. She tells the class about her idea and asks if anyone can tell her a sentence using the word "definitely".

Little Sophie's hand shoots up confidently and she says: "The sky is definitely blue."

"No, Sophie," says the teacher. "The sky is not definitely blue, it can be grey and cloudy. Anyone else?" Callum's hand pops straight up and he proclaims: "The water is definitely clear." To which the teacher answers: "No, it's not, it can be blue or green." Then Craig, the shyest boy in the class, nervously raises his hand and asks: "If I fart, should it be lumpy?" "No," the teacher responds. So Craig says: "Then I've definitely crapped myself."

Nuts

A lucky escape

A man walks into a bar grinning his face off. "The beers are on me!" he says, happily. "My wife has just run off with my best friend."

"That's a shame," says the barman. "Why aren't you sad?"

"Sad?" asks the man. "They've saved me a fortune. They were both pregnant."

Marital relations

Mr Johnson and his secretary are on a first-class flight. As they're nodding off for the night, the secretary, who has long had a crush on her boss, says in her most seductive voice, "I'm a little cold. Can I get under your blanket?"

Reading her signals clearly, the boss says, "How would you like to be Mrs Johnson for a while?"

"I'd love it!" the secretary replies, jumping at the chance.

"Great," Mr Johnson says, "then get your own damn blanket."

Famous last words

What was the last thing Nelson said to his men before they got on the boat?

"Get on the boat."

Present laughter

Four brothers grow up to become wealthy doctors and lawyers. At a meal, they're discussing what gifts they're about to give their elderly mother for her birthday. The first brother pipes up, "I've had a big house built for her."

Another sibling chips in with, "Well, I've had a £100,000 cinema installed in that house for her."

"That's nothing," offers the third brother. "I had my car dealer deliver her a brand-new Ferrari Enzo."

The remaining brother finally speaks up: "You know how Mum loved reading the Bible, but she can't read so well these days? Well, I met this priest who has a parrot that recites the entire book! It took 12 years to teach him – and I've had to pledge to contribute £100,000 to the Church – but I've got him! Mum just has to name the chapter and verse and the parrot will recite it." The brothers are impressed.

Post-birthday, Mum pens some thank-you notes. "David, the house you built is so huge! I live in only one room, but I have to clean the whole place! Not great, but thanks anyway, son." To her second eldest she writes: "Michael, that cinema holds 50 people... but all my friends are dead! I'll never use it. Thank you for the gesture all the same." "Peter," she writes to her third eldest, "I'm too old to drive, so I never use the Enzo. The thought was kind. Thanks."

Finally, the youngest boy receives his letter: "Dearest Richard! You were the only son to have the good sense to put a little thought into your gift. The chicken was absolutely delicious!"

That's my boy!

Two old men are arguing about whose dog is smarter.

"My dog's practically a genius," the first fella boasts. "Every morning he waits patiently for the newspaper to be delivered and then brings it in to me."

"I know," the second fella replies.

"What do you mean?" the first man asks. "How do you know?"

The second man answers, "My dog told me about it."

Nuts

We'll never know

An ugly man walks into his local with a big grin on his face.

"Why so happy?" asks the barman.

"Well, you know I live by a railway," replies the ugly man.

"On my way home last night I noticed a woman tied to the tracks. I, of course, freed her, took her back to mine and, to cut a long story short, we made love all night."

"You lucky sod!" says the barman. "Was she pretty?"

"Dunno... never found the head!"

Screw you

What's the difference between a bad lawyer and a good lawyer?

A bad lawyer can let a case drag on for months.

A good lawyer can make it last for years.

The big boss

Who's the king of the hankies?
 The handkerchief.

The truth will out

A mum is driving her little girl to a friend's house to play.

"Mummy," the little girl asks. "How old are you?"

"You aren't supposed to ask a lady her age," the mother warns. "It's personal and it is not polite."

"OK," the little girl says. "Why did you and Daddy get a divorce?"

"That's enough questions. Honestly!" exclaims the exasperated mother, before walking away as the two friends begin to play.

"My mum wouldn't tell me anything," the little girl says to her friend.

"Well," said the friend. "All you need to do is look at

her birth certificate. It has everything on it."

Later that night, the little girl says to her mother, "I know how old you are. You're 32."

The mother is surprised and asks, "How did you find that out?"

"And," the little girl says, triumphantly, "I know why you and Daddy got a divorce."

"Oh, really?" the mother asks, somewhat surprised. "And why's that?"

"Because you only got an F in sex."

Spicy

Did you hear about the guy in hospital for sniffing curry powder?

He's in a korma.

Nuts

That's telling her

Little Tommy is sitting on a park bench, stuffing a bag of pick-and-mix into his mouth, when an old lady comes over to tell him off. "Son, don't you know that eating all those sweets will rot your teeth and make you sick?"

"My grandfather lived to be 105 years old!" replies Tommy.

"Did he always eat a whole bag of sweets in one go?" the old lady retorts.

"No," answers Tommy, "but he did mind his own business."

Nuts

A fate worse than death

An Englishman, a Frenchman and a German survive a plane crash. They are stranded on a desert island and, knowing that nothing but certain death is to be their fate, God grants them one last wish. The Frenchman asks for a huge, sumptuous dinner washed down with an excellent Burgundy; the German asks if he can make the after-dinner speech; and the Englishman clasps his hands together and says: "Please, God, let me die before the German starts."

Good job

Somebody complimented me on my driving the other day. They left me a note on my windscreen saying, "Parking Fine."

Secret shame

Little David was in his primary class when the teacher asked the children what their fathers did for a living. All the typical answers came up: fireman; policeman; salesman. David was being uncharacteristically quiet, so the teacher asked him about his father. "My father's an exotic dancer in a gay cabaret and he takes off all his clothes in front of other men," he replied.

The teacher, obviously shaken by this statement, took little David aside to ask him, "Is that really true about your father?" "No," said David. "He plays for Tottenham Hotspur, but I was too embarrassed to say that in front of the other kids."

Fair question

The instructor at a pregnancy and labour class is teaching the young couples how to breathe properly during delivery. The teacher announces, "Ladies, exercise is good for you. Walking is especially beneficial. And, gentlemen, it wouldn't hurt you to take the time to go walking with your partner." The room falls quiet. Finally, a man in the middle of the group raises his hand.

"Is it all right if she carries a golf bag while we walk?"

Nuts

Fringe benefits

A bloke goes into the Jobcentre in London and spots a job vacancy which reads, "Wanted: single man, willing to travel, must have own scissors. £500 a week guaranteed, plus company car and all expenses."

It sounds a bit too good to be true, so the bloke fronts up at the counter and quotes the job's reference number.

"Oh, that one," says the clerk. "It's a modelling agency here in London. They're looking for a pubic hair snipper. They supply girls who model underwear and before they go on the catwalk they report to you to snip off any wisps of pubic hair that are showing.

It pays well, but there are drawbacks; it involves a lot of travel to exotic places and you have to get used to living in first-class hotels."

"Well, I'd still like to apply," says the bloke.

The clerk says, "OK, here's an application form and a rail ticket to Manchester."

"What do I wanna go to Manchester for?"

"Well," says the clerk, "that's where the end of the queue is at the moment."

Crush puppy

How do you make a dog drink?
Put it in the liquidizer.

Hard to spot

A small boy is lost, so he goes up to a policeman and says, "I can't find my dad."

"What's he like?" the policeman enquires.

"Beer and women," replies the boy.

Making dough

The owner of a family-run bakery was being questioned by the Inland Revenue about his tax return, having reported a net profit of £45,000 for the year.

"Why don't you people leave me alone?" the baker said.

"I work like a dog, everyone in my family helps out and the place is only closed three days a year. And you want to know how I made £45,000?"

"It's not your income that bothers us," the taxman said. "It's these deductions. You listed six trips to Bermuda for you and your wife."

"Oh, that?" the owner said, smiling. "I forgot to tell you – we also deliver."

Size is everything

What did the elephant say to the naked man?
 It's cute, but can you pick up peanuts with it?

Judgemental

What do you call a judge with no thumbs?
    Justice Fingers.

Say knock knock

"Knock, knock."
  "Who's there?"
  "Control freak. Now this is where you say,
  'Control freak who?'"

Beggars can't be choosers

Two friends were playing golf when one pulled out a cigar.

He didn't have a lighter, so he asked his friend if he had one.

"Yep," he replied and pulled out a 12-inch Bic lighter from his golf bag.

"Wow!" said his friend. "Where did you get that monster?"

"I got it from the genie in my golf bag."

"You have a genie? Could I see him?"

The other bloke opens his golf bag and out pops a genie.

The friend asks the genie, "Since I'm a friend of

your master, will you grant me one wish?"

"Yes, I will," the genie replies. The friend asks the genie for a million bucks and the genie hops back into the golf bag and leaves him standing there, waiting for his million bucks.

Suddenly, the sky darkens and the sound of a million ducks flying overhead is heard.

The friend tells his golfing partner, "I asked for a million bucks, not a million ducks!"

He answers, "I forgot to say; he's a bit deaf. Do you really think I asked him for a 12-inch Bic?"

Step on it

A policeman got out of his car and the lad who was stopped for speeding rolled down his window. "I've been waiting for you all day," the policeman said.

"Yeah," replied the lad. "Well, I got here as fast as I could."

You've gotta be joking

An Englishman, an Irishman, a Scotsman, a Catholic, a Jew and a blind man walk into a pub. The landlord says: "Is this some kind of joke?"

Investor in people

An office manager arrives at his department and sees an employee sitting behind his desk, totally stressed out.

He gives him a spot of advice: "I went home every afternoon for two weeks and had myself pampered by my wife. It was fantastic and it really helped me. Maybe you should give it a try, too."

Two weeks later, when the manager arrives at his department, he sees the same man happy and full of energy at his desk. The faxes are piling up and the computer is running at full speed.

"Excellent," says the manager, "I see you followed my advice."

"I did," answers the employee. "It was great! By the way, I didn't know you had such a nice house!"

The best policy

A policeman pulls over a car for swerving and asks the driver to take a breathalyzer test.

"I can't do that," says the man. "I'm an asthmatic. The breathalyzer could bring on an attack."

So the policeman suggests a urine sample.

"Can't do it," says the man. "I'm a diabetic, so my urine always has strange stuff in it."

"Well," says the angry policeman, "why don't you just get out of the car and walk along this white line?"

"Sorry," says the man, "but I can't do that either."

"Why not?" asks the officer. "Because I'm drunk."

Far-fetched

There are two grains of sand in the desert.

One turns to the other and says, "Busy here, isn't it?"

Fairy tale

What did Cinderella say when she left Boots?

"Some day my prints will come."

Struck down in his prime

A man tells his doctor he's unable to do all the things round the house that he used to. After an examination, he says, "Tell me in plain English what's wrong with me, Doc."

"Well, in layman's terms, you're lazy," says the doctor.

"OK. Now give me a medical term, so I can tell my wife."